GOD Loves <u>YOU</u> <u>Exactly</u> As You Are!

GOD

Loves <u>YOU</u>
<u>Exactly</u> As You Are!

Understanding & Experiencing
Unconditional Divine Love

By Wade Galt

Possibility Infinity Publishing

To GOD...

*My Creator and the One Being Who
Completely Loves and Accepts Me
Exactly As I Am, Without Judgment,
Without Condition, and Without Exception.*

Unconditional Love:

Love _without_ Condition.

These Ideas Work For Me...

I wouldn't call them beliefs because I'm not attached to them. I'm not ready to kill or die to prove I'm right or that someone else is wrong. This is not dogma, so there's no need for anyone to argue. I'm not suggesting I'm right or others are wrong. I may be incorrect. I'm not saying I hold the only truth, the ultimate truth, or even truth.

This book is a collection of ideas that feel true to me, that inspire me, and that work for me (based on what I can see in my life). I'd love to hear how these and other ideas work for you. I see this as a two-way learning relationship that we can both learn from. I'm not the teacher. You're not the student. We're just two people exploring ideas about the divine in hope of improving our lives and the world.

Please Accept My Humility and My Grandiosity

It is my only intention that this work brings you closer to peace, love, joy, happiness, and a greater connection with the divine. Please excuse my limitations as a writer as I attempt to do this. It is not my intention to make anyone feel wrong, uncomfortable, that they need to change, or feel anything other than fully loved, accepted and supported.

Please accept my grandiosity in wanting to address such a huge and important subject (and any apparent presumption that I'm right). Please also accept my humility in doing my best to make myself vulnerable by sharing something I think will make the world a better place. I honor all those people, organizations, religions, beliefs, rituals, and everything else that seeks to do the same,

At the same time, I remain excited, open-hearted and open-minded to seeing how we may grow, evolve, and change how we relate with the divine and each other to bring about even more peace, love, and happiness.

An Invitation

We humans have created many rules, rituals, and practices, that center around our relationship with God (or whatever name you prefer for the divine).

Our intentions to express to God our gratitude, joy, inspiration, and happiness are certainly divine; however, it appears we humans sometimes get caught up in the details of the beliefs we have about God.

We seem to need to make ourselves right and others wrong, which causes heartache, pain, and sometimes death. It is possibly now more critical than ever that we learn to see each other with divine rather than human eyes. Our day-to-day happiness depends on this, and ultimately so might our existence.

If we can remember that it is we who made up the many rules and beliefs we have about the divine, we may be able to get past the chaos and pain of our judgmental (human) minds and find the love and peace of our unconditionally loving (divine) hearts. This book is an invitation to do so.

It is, of course, possible that God does not love us exactly as we are. I look to prove nothing with this work. I simply seek to share the joy and love I have experienced and hope that it inspires and changes your life the way it has changed mine.

Read Slowly...
Let It Sink In...
And Enjoy!

God Loves You Exactly as You Are!

God Made You Exactly as You Are!

God Makes Wonderful

Things!

And God Knows You are Wonderful!

God Loves You Exactly as You Are!

You Don't Have to Do Anything for God to Love You!

God Knows You Do Your Best!

God Loves You Exactly as You Are!

You Don't Have to Say Anything for God to Love You!

God Knows Your Every Thought, and Words are Not Necessary!

God Loves You Exactly as You Are!

You Don't Have to Know Anything for God to Love You!

You Don't Have to Believe Anything for God to Love You!

God Loves You Exactly as You Are!

You Don't Have to Give Anything for God to Love You!

God Has Enough Money and Things Already!

God Loves You Exactly as You Are!

You Don't Have to Eat or Not Eat Certain Foods for God to Love You!

God Created Everything, and Everything is Divine!

You Don't Have to Treat Certain Days as Special for God to Love You!

God Breathes Life and Love Into Every Day, and Every Day God Gives Us is Holy!

God Loves You Exactly as You Are!

You Don't Have to Keep Your Clothes on for God to Love You!

God Created the Human Body, and It Is Divine!

God Loves You Exactly as You Are!

You Don't Have to Be Faithful to Anything or Anyone for God to Love You!

Your Infidelities Hurt You and Those Around You, Not God!

God Loves You Exactly as You Are!

You Don't Have to Go or Be Anywhere for God to Love You!

God Knows Where to Find You!

God Loves You Exactly as You Are!

You Don't Have to Read Any Specific Books for God to Love You!

God Loves Those Who Can Read, Those Who Can't, and Those Who Don't!

God Loves You Exactly as You Are!

You Don't Have to Belong to a Certain Group for God to Love You!

God Loves All Groups and All Individuals for All are God's Creations!

God Loves You Exactly as You Are!

You Don't Have to Believe in God for God to Love You!

God and God's Existence are Not Threatened by What You Do or Do Not Believe!

God Loves You Exactly as You Are!

You Don't Have to Be Good for God to Love You!

God Knows Exactly Why You Do What You Do and Accepts You Fully Just As You Are!

God Loves You Exactly as You Are!

You Don't Have to Be Polite for God to Love You!

God Loves People With Great Manners and People Who Are Rude!

God Loves You Exactly as You Are!

You Don't Have to

Be Honest for God

to Love You!

God Knows the Truth and Lying Doesn't Hurt God!

Lying Only Hurts You and Those Around You.

God Loves You Exactly as You Are!

You Don't Have to Be Loving for God to Love You!

God Has Enough Love to Fill the Entire Universe!

God Loves You Exactly as You Are!

God Doesn't Need

Anything from You!

God Has Everything
God Needs!

God Loves You Exactly

as You Are!

You Don't Have to Worship or Praise God for God to Love You!

God Has High Self-Esteem and Doesn't Need Compliments to Feel Loving!

God Loves You Exactly as You Are!

You Don't Have to Wear Special Clothes for God to Love You!

God Knows the True Beauty of Who You Are On the Inside.

God Loves You Exactly as You Are!

You Don't Have to Be in Good Physical Shape for God to Love You!

God Loves All People –

Tall and Short,

Thick and Thin!

God Loves You Exactly as You Are!

You Don't Have to Be Born in a Certain Race or Ethnic Group for God to Love You!

God Created Diversity,

And Diversity is Divine!

God Loves All of God's Creations, and All People are God's Chosen People!

God Loves You Exactly as You Are!

God's Love for Us is So Unbelievably Amazing, Infinitely Powerful, and All-Accepting that We Can't Even Begin to Understand It.

God Loves You Even When You Lie, Cheat, and Steal!

Your Lying, Cheating, and Stealing Hurt You and Those Around You, Not God!

God Loves You Exactly as You Are!

God Loves You Even When You Curse and Swear!

God's Name Cannot Be Desecrated by You for It is Infinitely Divine!

God Loves You Exactly as You Are!

God Loves You Even When You are Angry with God!

God Does Not Take Things Personally.

God Takes Things Divinely!

God Loves You Exactly as You Are!

God Loves You Even When You are Hurtful Towards Others!

Your Actions Do Not Hurt God, But Only You and Those Around You!

God Loves You Exactly as You Are!

God Loves You Even When You Do Things You May Not Be Very Proud Of or Even Those Things You Are Ashamed Of!

God's Love Transcends Human Understanding and Human Capacity!

God Loves You Exactly as You Are!

God Loves the People We Call Criminals, Bums, Addicts, Villains, Victims, and Everyone Else.

God's Love Transcends Human Understanding and Human Capacity!

God Loves Us All

Exactly as We Are!

Just Because We Judge, Doesn't Mean God Judges.

God's Love Transcends Human Understanding and Human Capacity!

God Loves Us All Exactly as We Are!

Just Because We Can't Accept, Doesn't Mean God Can't Accept.

God's Love Transcends Human Understanding and Human Capacity!

God Loves Us All Exactly as We Are!

Just Because Our Love is Based on Conditions, Doesn't Mean God's Is.

God's Love Transcends Human Understanding and Human Capacity!

God Loves Us All

Exactly as We Are!

Just Because Our Love

Is Limited,

Doesn't Mean God's

Love Is Limited.

God's Love Transcends Human Understanding and Human Capacity!

God Loves Us All Exactly as We Are!

When We Can Learn to Love and Accept Ourselves Fully and Without Condition, We Can Love Like God Loves.

Then We Can Love Others As We Love Ourselves!

Then We Can Love Ourselves Exactly as We Are!

After Thoughts and Suggested Use

It may be that our greatest need as human beings is to feel loved. We look to our friends, our families, our co-workers, and even the people we meet on the streets to show us signs that they accept us and love us for who we are.

Many people take advantage of this desire to feel loved and use love as a weapon, withhold love unless their demands are met, and engage in other behaviors that manipulate us when we desperately need to feel loved.

Such behavior can lead us to feel unloved, unlovable, or at best – conditionally lovable or loved.

The divine is probably the only being that fully loves us and accepts us as we are, all the time, no matter what.

Use this simple book as a reminder anytime you find yourself feeling anything less than 1000% fully lovable, and if you like, share it with others.

Love and Acceptance, Good and Evil

Within this book, I have made reference to God accepting us even as we engage in behaviors and acts that many people consider "evil." I don't pretend to know where the line between "good" and "evil" exists in God's eyes, if in fact there is such a line for God. Many of the things I have mentioned may not be for "the greater good" of all, and many of them may not be very "loving" things to do. All of that being said, ***the issue of whether or not we are loved by the divine is a different issue from whether or not the divine would like to see us engage in certain types of behaviors and / or not engage in others***.

Just like a mother can love her child fully, even though that child does something she does not agree with, the divine can still love us while we do "unloving" things.

When people feel unloved or unnoticed, they will often do "negative" or "unloving" things to get attention. If they receive "negative" attention, they often continue doing these same things, simply because they want some type of attention. If, however, people feel loved and noticed, there is much less need for them to do such things.

Unconditional love has the power to heal all wounds. God is that love. Our judgments about what is "good" or "evil" are simply our human way of expressing what we desire to create and what we don't wish to create. Nothing proves ours judgments are correct. If *we can simply let God be the judge of what is good and what is bad, as many spiritual and religious traditions suggest, we can focus on simply loving and accepting one another.*

If we humans do not judge one another, and if it turns out that God does love us unconditionally, then there would be no judgment at all.

It is possible that all of our ideas of judgment, condemnation, and hell are our creations – not God's. If this is the case, then we can stop fighting for God's love, approval, and attention. Then, maybe we can focus on just being loving – unconditionally loving – and we can finally experience a glimpse of what it feels like to be divine.

God and Self-Esteem

It is possible that all our attempts to receive approval and love from others are really attempts to receive love from our creator. It's also possible that unless we feel loved by God that we will never be able to truly feel loved by others. After all, if the most loving being in the universe does not accept or love us, who would?

Much of modern psychology focuses on the power our relationships with our parents have in influencing our self-esteem and how we think about ourselves. Very often, deep relationship healing with our parents leads to significant transformations in our other relationships because we may tend to play out the problems of our relationship with our parents in other relationships and repeat the same unproductive patterns with others. Once we can shift one relationship, others usually follow.

While psychology has made great strides in the area of parent-child relationships, it is possible that *to truly create powerful and lasting healing, we may need to examine the "most primary" of all our relationships – our relationship with our divine creator.*

People sometimes ask me why I have such a high opinion of myself. I know that a huge reason is that my parents always told me how much they love me and how special I am. I now also see how my relationship with God has contributed even more powerfully to my high self-esteem. I don't know if my mother taught me that God loves me infinitely or if I simply knew that with sage-like child wisdom and she reinforced it, but either way I knew it, and I know it.

From there, I guess it's very simple. I know, at the deepest core of my being, that God loves me EXACTLY as I am. I know that more surely than I know whether or not the sun will rise tomorrow. Regardless of whether or not the sun rises tomorrow, I know God loves me EXACTLY as I am. Everything else, as Einstein might say, is a detail.

I Know

I know I have stability and security,
but sometimes forget.

I know I am prosperous and abundant,
but sometimes forget.

I know I am kind and loving,
but sometimes forget.

I know I am good and perfect as I am,
but sometimes forget.

I know I already have everything I think I need,
but sometimes forget.

I know God loves me exactly as I am,
and I never forget that.

All I have to do is stay conscious of that,
and I will remember everything else.

It's that simple.

Acknowledgments

Thank you God… for everyone and everything in my life. I am so blessed.

My intention is that all who read this book, including myself, will experience the joy, bliss and fulfillment that come from loving you, being loved by you, and knowing just how much we are loved by you.

About the Author

Wade has led retreats and personal growth workshops, authored books on spirituality, personal growth, finance, parenting, business growth & more.

He has worked successfully as a life coach, 4-day work week mentor, organizational consultant, computer trainer, sales consultant, executive coach, speaker, mental health counselor, management consultant, software designer and programmer, author, business analyst, financial counselor, and in many other capacities.

Wade has a Bachelor's degree in Marketing and a Master's degree in Mental Health Counseling Psychology.

He lives happily with his wife and children.

His email address is wade@wadegalt.com .

Author Blog & Website

You may visit Wade's blog & website at www.wadegalt.com.

Also by Wade Galt

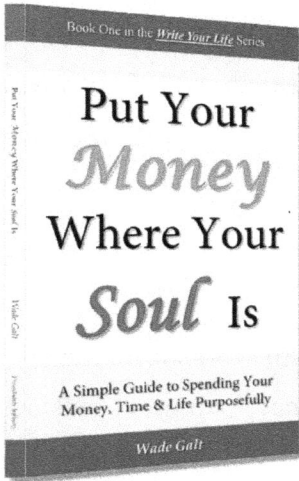

Put Your Money Where Your Soul Is

A Simple Guide to Spending Your Money, Time and Life Purposefully

Learn how to free up additional time, money and energy by redefining your relationships with money, time, people, and things.

Simple strategies, exercises & tools help you make powerful changes with very little effort or struggle.

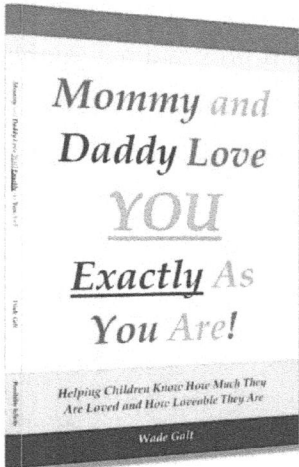

Mommy and Daddy Love You Exactly As You Are!

Helping Children Know How Much They Are Loved and How Loveable They Are

My hope is that this book helps you...

1) Let your child or children know how special they are.

2) Remember how special your child or children are.

3) Understand how much your parents love(d) you, whether or not they ever shared this with you.

The *God Equals Love* Book Series

(Free eBook Versions Available for All Books)

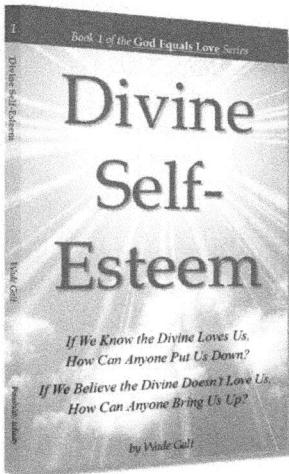

Book 1 - Divine Self-Esteem

Learning to Love Ourselves
the Way the Divine Loves Us

If we know the Divine loves us, how can anyone put us down?

If we believe the Divine doesn't love us, how can anyone bring us up?

Learn to see yourself through divinely loving eyes and catch a glimpse of the divinely-made miracle you are.

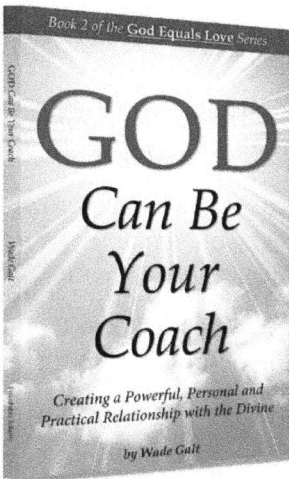

Book 2 - GOD Can Be Your Coach

Creating a Powerful, Personal and
Practical Relationship with the Divine

Create More Joy, Happiness, Love, Peace and Purpose in Your Life.

Learn One Simple Way to form a more powerful connection & relationship.

If You Knew You Could Connect with the Divine Anytime You Choose to Receive Guidance, Support, and Peace, Would You?

Will You?

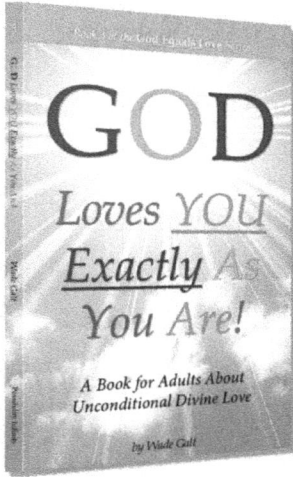

3 - GOD Loves You Exactly As You Are!

Understanding & Experiencing
Unconditional Divine Love

An Invitation to Consider & Experience the Life-Altering Understanding That You are Completely and Unconditionally Loved and Loveable EXACTLY AS YOU ARE!

What If God Loves You EXACTLY as You are?

How Would Understanding that Transform Your Life?

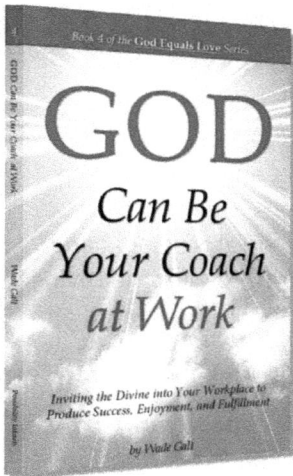

Book 4 - GOD Can Be Your Coach at Work

Inviting the Divine into Your Workplace to Produce Success, Enjoyment & Fulfillment

Few of us fully live our highest spiritual values in our workplace.

This is a source of frustration, shame, guilt & dissatisfaction for billions of us.

What if the divine actually wants us to experience life, love, joy, fulfillment, and abundance inside and outside our work?

What if the divine cares about our work simply because the divine cares for us?

This book is an invitation to work WITH the divine to create divinely inspired results for you and the world.

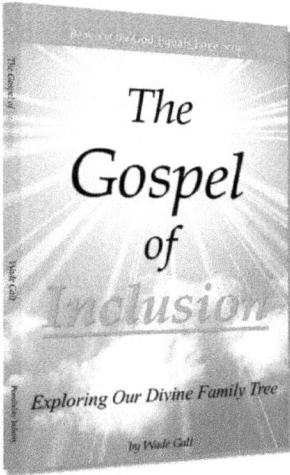

Book 5 - The Gospel of Inclusion

Exploring Our Divine Family Tree

Who is included in God's plan? Is it only people like me? Only people like you? What atrocities & apathy do we justify daily by declaring others are outside of God's chosen circle of people?

What if we really are part of one divine family? What would that mean? How would we have to change?

WARNING! Reading this book may lead you to (1) consider the possibility that we're all God's children and (2) do something about that. Proceed at your own risk!

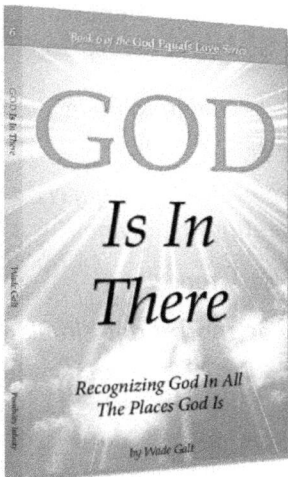

Book 6 - God Is In There

Recognizing God In All The Places God Is

If you could teach only one spiritual lesson, what would you teach?

What truth could you share that is so powerful, it would fundamentally transform the way others live?

There are a few core ideas that most spiritual traditions hold as true. Some believe that the most powerful and life-transforming truths are so self-evident and so obvious that all traditions agree about them.

This book contains one of those ideas.

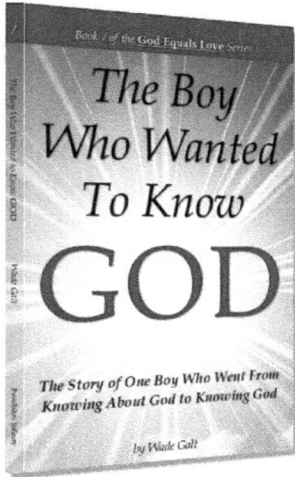

7 - The Boy Who Wanted to Know God

The Story of One Boy Who Went from Knowing About God to Knowing God

What would you be willing to do in order to meet God?

Join a curious and excited young boy on his journey to meeting the divine.

You might meet God, too.

The journey may be shorter and simpler than you think.

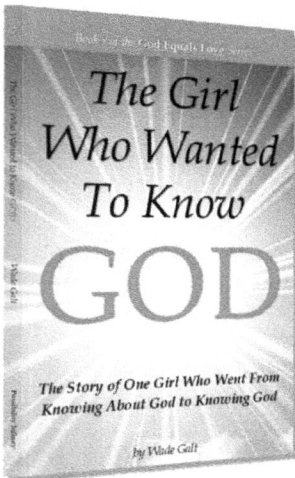

7 - The Girl Who Wanted to Know God

The Story of One Girl Who Went from Knowing About God to Knowing God

What would you be willing to do in order to meet God?

Join a curious and excited young girl on her journey to meeting the divine.

You might meet God, too.

The journey may be shorter and simpler than you think.

Other Books & Translated Books

Many of these books have been translated into Spanish, and there are other books also available.

To see these books and other books not listed here, visit www.wadegalt.com/books .

All profits from the sale of the GOD EQUALS LOVE books go to organizations and charities that seek to end unnecessary hunger and poverty.

New Book & Program Notifications

If you'd like to be emailed when we release new books, audios and other programs please visit www.wadegalt.com/notifiy to sign up for these notifications.

Share the Message & the Love

I hope this helps you see & feel how truly amazing and miraculous of a creation you are and how much the divine values you.

If you found the book to be helpful, would you please be so kind as to write a review on Amazon for the book or share the book on Facebook, Instagram, Twitter or other social media so others may benefit from it as well?

Even if it's a super-short review, every little bit helps.

Thank you so much.

If there's anything I can do to help you further with this work, please email me at is wade@wadegalt.com .

All my best,

Wade

www.ingramcontent.com/pod-product-compliance
Lightning Source LLC
Chambersburg PA
CBHW070637030426
42337CB00020B/4057